BÉJART
BY
BÉJART

BÉJART
BY
BÉJART

Photographed,
conceived, and designed
by
Colette Masson
Jean-Louis Rousseau
and
Pierre Faucheux

Handwritten comments
by Maurice Béjart

Translations by Richard Miller

CONGDON & LATTÈS, INC.
NEW YORK

We would like to thank

Maurice Huismann,
Director, Théâtre Royale de la Monnaie, Brussels,

Anne Lotsy,
Administrator, Ballet of the Twentieth Century;

Sonia Mandel,

Pierre and Louba Dobriévich;

Judith Gombar, Joëlle Roustan, Roger Bernard, and
Thierry Bosquet, stage designers;

and to express our gratitude to all the
artists of the Ballet of the Twentieth Century, without whom
this book could not have been
undertaken or successfully accomplished.

To Jorge Donn

From Wagner
to Fellini

In the nineteenth century, opera reigned supreme. What drama had been for the seventeenth century, opera was for the new era: the theatrical spectacle *par excellence*. Yet within a very short time, composers began to pander to the desires of their audience: the subject ceased to matter and became merely the pretext for a succession of set pieces—arias, duets, trios, ensembles with chorus—which together formed the sacrosanct framework of the genre. Opera came under the control of the singers, to be formed by their particular gifts, their likes and dislikes. Wagner turned his back on this decadent state of affairs. A poet, dramatist, and musician, he conceived of opera not as an entertainment but as a total means of expression, a *Gesamtkunstwerk,* in which he alone would control the action, the words, and the vocal line. He worked toward a completely unified end product because he himself had a unified vision of the world; thus each of his operas, however lengthy, is only a fragment of a single and unique work, one stage in a journey that leads from the apparition of the ghostly vessel of *The Flying Dutchman* to the Grail of *Parsifal.*

In short, Wagner added the demands of an architect to those of the poet, the dramatist, and the musician. He refused to allow his work to be performed in a setting unsuited to its nature, its expressive purpose. Bayreuth is not a theater in the Italian style with stalls, tiers of boxes, and a balcony for the lower classes—mirroring the social hierarchy—but rather a Grecian amphitheater, a place for collective celebration. The only important thing is the mystery of the work performed within it. Wagner's creative genius, however, did not extend to scenery; it was not until seventy years after his death that his grandson Wieland removed from his stage the painted flats that had encroached upon it: under Wieland's direction, the costumes and scenery took on the purity of elemental signs and the lighting acquired a dramatic function that enabled the work to expand and unfold in one continuous vision. Long before this final step was achieved, however, opera had ceased to enjoy its former audience and vitality.

At the beginning of the twentieth century, the Ballets Russes emerged, introducing dance as a vital art form. The effect was so startling, so powerful, that it altered the earlier concept of the dance as no more than a minor branch of theater. The magic of opera, of *Tristan and Isolde,* of *Parsifal,* was superseded by the enchantment of *Scheherazade* and *Firebird;* the emotion inspired by the celebration of a mystic rite was replaced by the excitement of sheer spectacle. The public was no longer moved, but dazzled. Awakening from Wagner's spell, spectators redis- covered their innocence, and the various arts, long forced by Wagner into one single expressive statement, regained their autonomy.

Diaghilev regarded ballet as an opportunity to combine music, painting, and dance; the stage was the arena where they joined together. In combining these elements, in coaxing their interaction to produce fruitful results, he relied upon his own taste: *Afternoon of a Faun* and *Daphnis and Chloë* brought together Debussy and Bakst, Bakst and Ravel; *The Three-Cornered Hat, Pulcinella,* and *Les Noces* brought together Falla and Picasso, Picasso and Stravinsky, Stravinsky and Gontcharova; in his ballets Diaghilev introduced choreographers and dancers like Fokine, Massine, and Nijinsky. In the end, however, the success of such an undertaking depends upon the quality of the collaboration and on its constant renewal.

Long after Diaghilev's death, only Balanchine and Stravinsky continued to collaborate: although their work together became more abstract, distancing itself from the luxury of the Ballets Russes, it nevertheless remains an example of perfect equality between music and dance—as exemplified by *Agon.* Thanks to Diaghilev and his accomplishments, to the series of works he inspired, ballet has become the twentieth century's theatrical spectacle *par excellence.* And like opera in the nineteenth century, it too has fallen prey to routine, to mere technical display.

In 1955, Maurice Béjart's *Symphony for a Man Alone,* a ballet of compelling brutality, not only revealed a new aesthetics of dance (new in every way: in attitude, in gesture, in movement, sound, and scenery) but made new demands, of which aesthetic effect was merely an external manifestation. For Béjart, dance is a total means of expression, a vehicle for the whole being, for all emotions and thoughts, the rival of music and poetry. He thus does not regard his work as a series of unrelated ballets, of finished and separate entities representing discrete events; on the contrary, he sees each ballet as a fragment of a work in progress, as a stage in a journey toward an unknown destination, a page from a journal in which he daily continues to write. Choreography becomes, therefore, what its name implies: the writing of a man for whom dance is a language.

Béjart has drawn inspiration from a variety of sources: a poem by Petrarch or Saâdi, St. John of the Cross or Nietzsche, Baudelaire or Cocteau; a score by Bach or Beethoven, Mahler or Richard Strauss, Boulez or Stockhausen. Dance becomes an incarnation: of characters, themes, symbols, and visions, as embodied in *I Trionfi* or *Golestan,* in *The Dark Night* or *Zarathustra,* in *Les Fleurs du Mal* or *The Angel Heurtebise;* it is the incarnation of the emotion expressed in a cantata, a symphony, or a song cycle, as in the pure instrumental and vocal combination of *Le Marteau sans Maître* or in the solo voices of *Stimmung*.

Béjart has thereby transformed the nature and function of ballet: his *Ninth Symphony* is a danced concert, as is *Actus Tragicus; Mass for the Present Time,* like *Bhakti,* is a rite, as are *Stimmung* and *The Conquerors; The Dark Night* and *The Angel Heurtebise* combine choreography and stage direction, actor and dancer. And just as Béjart demands that the various artistic disciplines blend into a single expressive whole, mingling words and music, basing movement on the rhythms of a sacred text as easily as on the ticking of a metronome, breaking down the barriers between different kinds of stage spectacle in order to arrive at one limitless spectacle, so too he rejects the separation between stage and audience, placing his stage in the midst of the spectators, turning his back on the conventions of the Italian-style theater and even of theater itself. And to achieve the union between this dance and a new public, he chooses to perform in amphitheaters, in circus tents and sports arenas, in parks and public squares—dance is created by relationships: between time and space, music and architecture, heart and body, man and the universe, man and man.

So Béjart has moved away from the ballet as conceived by Diaghilev. Although he derives the basic material of *Bacchanale, Mathilde,* and *The Conquerors* from Wagner (from *Tannhäuser,* the *Wesendonck Lieder,* and *Tristan and Isolde*) the inspiration he takes from the composer is very general: Béjart's goal is to construct a whole and continuous work from whatever sources, notwithstanding the nature or form of its separate parts; his desire is to express his vision of the world by means of universal themes and symbols, to give each of his spectacles the quality of a collective celebration.

And it is along these lines that his work, from ballet to ballet, has in fact developed. The celebration of the *élan vital* in *The Rite of Spring* leads into the first two movements of *The Ninth Symphony* and the opening episode of *Golestan.* The trials to which the soul submits, in *The Voyage,* on its way to a new existence, matches the testing of the central figure in *The Conquerors* as he seeks fulfillment in love. The final sequence of *Mass for the Present Time* leads toward the final vision of *I Trionfi:* in the silence of these two episodes we find the same detachment, the same serenity—perhaps even the same expectation.

And Woman as Béjart envisages her—is she not alternately Isolde and Salome? We find her as Mathilde and as Erotica, as the Queen of the Night in *The Conquerors* and as the solar Eve in *Le Marteau sans Maître;* while another creature, more spiritual than carnal, inspires the poetic ideal of the Girl in Pink for *Nijinsky* and Laura for Petrarch.

The young man through whom Béjart expresses the permanence of childhood and the accession of the human being to a world of grace and love is, in turn, Romeo, the victim of *Can This Be Death?*, the Clown of God, the Wayfarer, the Poet of *I Trionfi*—and he is also the Angel Heurtebise, half dream and half reality, enchanter and tempter, as well as the Archangel Lucifer of *Our Faust*, an incarnation of ambiguity.

Detesting systematization, Béjart will turn to any discipline, but the cohesiveness of his work, its continuity, depends on the part played by the human body. He has stated that now, after many years during which the word has been all important, it is time to reinstate gesture as an expression of thought. Spectacle must rely henceforth upon the dance, which will take up where words and music leave off, revealing to us what speech is incapable of communicating.

To this end, Béjart has been a theatrical innovator: *The Damnation of Faust, The Tales of Hoffmann,* and *La Traviata* have become fragments of his personal opus. He gives free rein to the stimulus his plastic imagination receives from the music of Berlioz, from Hoffmann's universe, from the character of the Lady of the Camellias. He will sometimes combine dancers and singers in an attempt to escape outmoded conventions and to represent the inner lives of the characters: the souls of Faust and Marguerite as they escape the prison of their bodies and inevitable damnation; Stella, the female ideal the poet Hoffmann seeks during his unhappy adventures; the naked youth that Violetta (no longer a courtesan, but an artist) creates in order to realize her own vision. In his staging of such works, the choreography engenders a further, imaginary space in which form, movement, and gesture develop freely, without restraint, and by means of which Béjart is able to reveal the innermost nature of the characters in counterpoint to their outward appearance.

In 1962, with his staging of Stravinsky's *Les Noces*, Béjart had already begun to employ this new, gestural way of writing: dressed in heavy, ornate costumes, the bridal pair were seen as hierarchical figures, set apart from the excitement surrounding them, while dancers—the couple's embodied thoughts—dressed in white, traced out the signs of their emotions, their tenderness, modesty, and anxiety, in space.

As he gradually achieved an increasing fluency in this new mode of writing, Béjart began to create his own theater, to which every discipline made its contribution: Baudelaire, *Nijinsky, Our Faust, Le Molière Imaginaire.* In each instance a principal character drawn from history or fiction is made abstract, embodied in a single incarnation and then revealed, divided into multiple aspects by several interpreters, like a figure broken up in a faceted mirror each of whose surfaces reflects a different fragment of the total image: thus six poets create Baudelaire; Nijinsky, the Clown of God, is accompanied by dancers in four of his roles; the Aged Faust, lost in the world of his own magic, is encircled by twelve adolescent Fausts; the adult Molière encounters the young Molière, the author of his plays, his living avatar. In each ballet, Béjart has managed to capture the living being, not in his uniqueness but in his variety, powerfully projecting on the stage man's complexity, his experience, his passion.

But whether conceiving a spectacle as a unity or as a composite, whether developing his ballet with total rigor or with the wildest fantasy, whether making it stark or magnificent, whether employing pure dance alone or using every possible theatrical effect, Béjart has always based his work on the human body, the dancer's body. In it he finds not only his interpreter but his inspiration. He observes it, questions it, molds it; using it as his basic material, he invents. For him, this body is never an abstract entity, never merely an element of design (as it is for Balanchine); on the contrary, he considers the body in all its aspects, the single, unique body of each individual dancer, free in its powers of expression, of fascination, of provocation, to be at once an underlying motivating force for his work and a medium through which he can realize his aspirations as a choreographer.

It is for this reason that Béjart has not collaborated with painters: unlike Diaghilev, he rejects the notion that dance derives from the picture—from a painted masterpiece—and he excludes any decor not absolutely essential to an understanding of the work, anything that might, by its very quality, compromise the quality of the dance itself. No line may alter the line created by the movement; no ornament may be allowed to contradict the effectiveness of gesture. Béjart frequently uses lighting alone to enhance the dancer's body in all its nakedness.

His spectacles often rely as well upon another kind of collaboration: their physical settings, indoors or out, park, public square, amphitheater, or circus. And the decor can no longer be compared to a picture, restraining the dance within a frame: it is sometimes horizontal, sometimes vertical. The decor is the stage—it provides the stage—dividing it or enlarging it; and it forms a direct link between the dancer and the spectator that is also symbolic of the work itself. For *Romeo and Juliet* it is a shell inspired by the public square in Siena; for Baudelaire, a full-blown flower; for *Nijinsky,* a misshapen triangle; for *Golestan,* a pointed arch; for *I Trionfi,* a star shape. Dance thereby ceases to be perceived from the front, like painting; created in the midst of bleachers, in the midst of the audience, dance can be examined from every angle, like sculpture, of which dance is the animate twin.

From ballet to ballet, therefore, Béjart has created a portrait of Béjart himself: a choreographer, a theatrical craftsman, an inhabitant of a unique universe—as is seen in his *Loves of a Poet,* in which, eschewing any dramatic subtext, he indulges in introspection, usurps the role of literature, and translates his innermost throughts and feelings into a series of incarnate metaphors. It is thus natural that he should have much in common with Fellini. Both share the same irreverence and extravagance, a taste for circuses and celebrations, for clowns and Pierrots, for masques and travesty. They have the same fondness for sharp contrasts: nostalgia for purity and fascination with decadence, Franciscan naiveté and baroque fantasy, the slow, regular breath and the catch in the throat. And above all, they share the same mode of creation. Whether they employ Casanova's *Memoirs* or Nijinsky's *Journal,* both absorb their subjects in the same way that Stravinsky absorbed Pergolese—as visionaries rather than illustrators, altering their basic material and concerned solely with their intuition of human beings and objects, mastering all the means available to them—image and rhythm, face and body, costume and scenery, lighting and sound—so that the universe they reveal on the screen or on the stage seems to have emanated from their souls. Free and solitary creators, they have both set for themselves the same rule, the most demanding and perilous rule of all: to be constantly inventive.

Birth of a Book

In January 1970, the Ballet of the Twentieth Century gave a series of performances at the Palais de Chaillot in Paris. In the same month, an exhibit celebrating the company's tenth anniversary was mounted at Les Halles, under a tent erected in one of Baltard's pavilions. The exhibition opened one Sunday at noon. At that hour, I entered the tent; I was the first visitor—and, for a while, the only one. In silence, I was able to examine the huge photographs suspended from the girders—fragments of ballets with which I was already familiar but which I now saw broken down and rearranged, like sequences in a single, vast fresco. Suddenly I thought: what a marvelous book!

I rejected for several years the temptation to undertake it on my own. During those years Béjart continued to create ballets; the more copious his work grew, the more I began to fear that I would never be able to capture it. And so, in 1974, I decided to conquer my doubts: after all, I was not planning to write the man's biography, nor did I intend to make a complete inventory of his work. From the beginning, I knew what three elements the book should contain: photographs, quotations from the texts that had inspired Béjart, and the notes necessary for an understanding of the works. I saw the book as a tryptich, with a central panel in which certain ballets would be displayed—ballets chosen for their special characteristics, style, and meaning—framed by two outer panels, one of which would concentrate on a chronological approach to the work, the other on documents dealing with aspects of the performances.

Of course, any book would depend upon the quality of the photographs and design. Colette Masson's photographic perception of the ballets conformed with my own, based as it is on two contrasting demands: precision and movement. She rejects half measures because they cannot reveal truth. She re-creates Béjart's work as an incarnate universe, in which each emotion and thought is envisaged and embodied, just as she makes tangible the space of the mind itself, the mobility of the light. The acuity with which her eye has transfixed hair, facial expression, flesh, and gesture reveals the dancer as Béjart himself conceives him, not as a surrogate, but in all his actual, full being. She never contravenes the animating movement, the *raison d'être* of dance. In her photographs, precision becomes the basis for poetry.

As for the book design—I almost write "set design"—I could entrust it to no one but Pierre Faucheux, with whom I had long collaborated. My knowledge of his experiments and his achievements told me that he was first and foremost an architect—an architect of books. He has given the photographs, quotations, and notes a framework within which to move—a form, a proportion, and a rhythm—he has given them life.

We began working together in November 1974, when *I Trionfi* was being performed in Paris, and we concluded our labors in February 1979, during the performances of *Loves of a Poet*. In March 1976, we brought to Béjart—to the vast loft in Brussels where he lives—a dummy of the book. We were trying to persuade him to write his own comments in the margins, by hand, and to authorize us to reproduce them. He agreed, remarking only: "My handwriting isn't very attractive."

Jean-Louis Rousseau

Chronology

1955 Symphony for a Man Alone (Symphonie pour
un Homme Seul)

1961 Boléro

1965 Mathilde

1965 Erotica

1968 The Dark Night (La Nuit Obscure)

1970 Actus Tragicus

1971 Songs of a Wayfarer (Le Chant du
Compagnon Errant)

1973 Le Marteau sans Maître

1975 Pli selon Pli

L'homme et la femme, unis, mélangés, confondus, complices et ennemis, amants

Symphony for a Man Alone
Music by Pierre Schaeffer and Pierre Henry

Suzanne Farrell

et frères comme ces souverains Egyptiens divins et incestueux, enchevêtrés pour l'éternité.

Man and woman, joined, intertwined, blended, accomplices and enemies, lovers and siblings—like those divine and incestuous Egyptian rulers, intermingled for eternity.

Jorge Donn

15

Pythia on her tripod,
her body becomes oracle and
the universe of signs
leads us into the magic
of incantation.

Boléro
Music by Maurice Ravel

Maya Plisetskaya

The dance is a ritual.

Pythie sur son trépied,
son corps devient oracle et
l'univers des signes nous
entraine dans la magie
incantatoire .

La danse est un rite.

Mathilde
Music by Richard Wagner

Maryse Pâtris
Germinal Cassado
Pierre Dobriévich
Angèle Albrecht
Jorge Donn
Gérard Wilk

This struggle between the mirage
of baroque forms and the beauty of the simple,
unadorned body. The movement
of the multiple apparitions toward the
real, and the proof of abstract truth.

Cette lutte entre le mirage
des formes baroques et la
beauté du corps simple et
nu. Le mouvement des
apparitions multiples du
réel, et l'évidence de
la vérité abstraite.

Souviens toi que

je t'aime !

And remember that I love thee!

Erotica
Music by Tadeusz Baird

Suzanne Farrell   Daniel Lommel

The Dark Night
Poem by St. John of the Cross

Maria Casarès
Maurice Béjart

L'homme
La Femme
La Nuit
Le Jour
Divin
Profane
Parole
Geste ... etc ...

Man
Woman
Night
Day
Divine
Profane
Word
Gesture...etc....

And what if opposites were
only an illusion?

Et si les contraires
n'étaient qu'une illusion ?

Actus Tragicus
Music by Johann Sebastian Bach

Angèle Albrecht
Rita Poelvoorde
Jorge Lefèvre
Daniel Lommel
Andrzej Ziemski

Dance, writing,
Syntax, clarity,
Movement, breath,

24

Danse , écriture .
Syntaxe , clarté ,
Mouvement , respiration ,

conscience,   Effort,
simplicité,   ligne
Musique

conscience, effort,
simplicity, line, Music

Songs of a Wayfarer
Music by Gustav Mahler

Jorge Donn
Daniel Lommel

The Other is yet myself; here, too, the mirror is a key,
so long as we penetrate to the other side of that mirror.

L'autre est encore moi-même;
ici aussi le miroir est
une des clefs, à condition

de passer de l'autre côté
de ce miroir.

Aller au bout du mensonge
des apparences pour trouver...

Pass through the falsehood of appearances to find...

Le Marteau sans Maître*
Music by Pierre Boulez

Suzanne Farrell
Jorge Donn

Comme ces dessins abstraits qui s'enroulent, vegetation minerale, au fronton des Mosquées et se nomment...

Arabesques.

Like those abstract drawings
that unfurl—mineral vegetation—
across the facades of mosques,
and are known as…
Arabesques.

(N'est-il pas curieux que le nom
du plus beau mouvement de la
Danse occidentale vienne des
Arabes .)

(Isn't it odd that the name for the loveliest movement
in Western dance should come from the Arabs.)

Pli selon Pli*
Music by Pierre Boulez

Lynn Glauber
Ivan Marko
Andrzej Ziemski

*Literally, "Fold upon Fold."

I bring you the Child of an Idumean night
Stéphane Mallarmé

37

Silence

The Creation of an Opus

The Ninth Symphony

Music by Ludwig van Beethoven
Stage design and costumes by
Joëlle Roustan and Roger Bernard

First performance,
October 27, 1964,
at the Cirque Royale of Brussels

The photographs, taken in 1969 and 1975,
show the following soloists:

> Rita Poelvoorde
> Jan Nuyts
> Luciana Savignano
> Jorge Lefèvre
> Dyane Gray-Cullert
> Daniel Lommel
> Jorge Donn

The Ninth Symphony is an artistic expression of Beethoven's loftiest ideal, best described by his contemporary, Goethe: "We are members of that race which, out of darkness, aspires toward the light." Béjart has said that the choreography of *The Ninth Symphony* is based solely on the music itself. It is not a ballet in the traditional sense: it is a celebration of a work that is the property of all mankind, one not only played and sung, but danced—as was Greek tragedy.

In order to enhance the inherent nature of this collective ceremony, the stage design also departs from tradition: the orchestra pit has been done away with, creating as it does a barrier between dancers and audience; the orchestra and chorus are placed on risers at the back of the circular stage, which is set, like the dance it contains, in the midst of the spectators.

Béjart selected an appropriate color for each movement in order to accentuate the over-all progression of the work—from darkness toward light—and in order better to express its dual emotional message: the union of all men and the union of man with the universe. The colors symbolize both the races of man and the elements: brown, red, white, yellow.

Man verwandele das Beethovensche Jubellied der « Freude » in ein Gemälde und bleibe mit seiner Einbildungskraft nicht zurück, wenn die Millionen schauervoll in den Staub sinken : so kann man sich dem Dionysischen nähern.

Let us transform Beethoven's triumphant Hymn to Joy into a tableau, and, with the poet, see the multitudes prostrate upon the earth; thus, in thought, shall we attain the power of Dionysus.

41

First movement
Allegro ma non troppo
un poco maestoso

Second movement
Molto vivace

Third movement
Adagio molto e cantabile

Fourth movement
Finale, mit Schlusschor uber Schillers Ode
«an die Freude»

43

JOY!

La Joie ! Symphonie en quatre mouvements ... L'homme à travers les quatre éléments Terre, Feu, Eau, Air découvre sa vraie nature.

Joy! Symphony in four
movements... Man through
the four elements
Earth, Fire, Water, Air
discovers his true nature.

Stimmung

Music by Karlheinz Stockhausen
Stage design and costumes by
Joëlle Roustan and Roger Bernard

First performance,
December 13, 1972,
at the Université Libre of Brussels

The photographs, taken in 1975, show the
following performers:

> Hitomi Asakawa
> Jean-Marie Limon
> Jorge Donn
> Niklas Ek
> Dyane Gray-Cullert
> Dwight Lomont-Hugues
> Andrzej Ziemski
> Daniel Lommel
> Bertrand Pie
> Monet Robier
> Catherine Verneuil

Stockhausen composed *Stimmung* for six singers: two
sopranos, mezzo-soprano, tenor, baritone, and bass. The
work's German title can have a variety of meanings: the
tuning of true musical intervals, a mood or emotional
state, ambience. *Stimme,* the root word, means "voice."
Stockhausen chose the title for its very ambiguity, after
he had completed the score.
The music follows a kind of game in which each singer is
provided with eight or nine musical models and eleven
magic words that he or she is allowed to introduce into
the sound pattern at will, based on a formal scheme and
according to context. The other singers react to the
magic words with various digressions, pitch oscillations
or unison responses.
The choreography, like the music, is meditative—"a
spaceship speeding toward the cosmic and the divine,"
in the composer's words—with, as Béjart has said, the
sole aim of "prolonging in space, in tangible form," the
vocal vibrations that emanate "from man's absolute
center."
The magic words—names of a wide variety of divin-
ities—are accompanied by magical, but also commonplace, gestures: caresses, dances, embraces, grimaces,
greetings, gathering flowers, drawing water from a well,
working clay...
The ballet is a ceremony; it begins and ends with
breathing. Ten supine dancers form a perfect Pythag-
orean triangle containing the ten prime numbers which
form the basis of all mathematics. In a circular mirror
placed on the ground, an eleventh dancer contemplates
his reflection.

Between this beginning and this ending, a series of ritual
sequences creates a celebration of the commonplace,
based on the magical gestures, while each dancer takes
his turn at the mirror and questions his own image.

The stage design includes a platform draped in black at
the back of the stage on which the six vocalists are
seated in a circle around a lamp. The circular mirror is
placed at the left, stage front.

Il existe 99 Noms de Dieu
Nul ne connait le
centième qui est la clef
de la science, de la vie,
de l'Univers ...

God has 99 names. No one knows the
hundredth name, which is the key to science,
to life, to the Universe…

« Dieu très haut est beau,
il aime la beauté » – Mais il
est impossible d'accéder à la
beauté sans la Médiation de l'Amour »
— SOHRAWARDI —

"God on high is beautiful, he loves beauty—but
beauty cannot be achieved without the mediation of Love."
Sohrawardi

Bismillah —

Vishnu
Tangaroa
Usi-Afu
Uranus
Uwoluwo
Hera

Rhea
Elohim
Munganagana
Ahura Mazda

Usi-Neno
Aeolus
Abassi-Abumo
Geb
Hina-a-tuatua-a-kakai

Tamoi

Isis
Elyon
Nut
Viracocha

Grogoragally
Tamosei

Atum-ra
Rangi
Uitzilopochtli
Yahweh
Varuna
Venus
Mulugu
Tlaloc
Sussistinako
Sedna

Can This Be Death?

Music by Richard Strauss

First performance,
April 4, 1970,
at the Opéra of Marseilles

The photographs, taken in 1976,
show the following performers:

> Jorge Donn
> Angèle Albrecht
> Lynn Glauber
> Shonach Mirk
> Catherine Verneuil

Strauss composed his final work, the *Four Last Songs,* to three poems by Hermann Hesse ("In Spring," "September," "While Going to Sleep") and one by Eichendorff ("At Sunset").

Like *Capriccio,* the *Oboe Concerto,* and the *Metamorphosen* for string orchestra, the *Four Last Songs* eschews the exuberant, the forceful: the music is serene and refined, with a melancholy more poignant for being understated—an autumnal music that faces death unafraid, with a kind of tenderness. From this acutely personal score Béjart has drawn the substance of his ballet: a man at the threshold of death re-encounters the four women he has loved during his life.

Three of them had shared periods of his life; the fourth is a woman he had only glimpsed. Yet she is the one who will accompany him at the end: can this be death?

The ballet's title is taken from the final line of Eichendorff's poem: *"Ist dies etwa der Tod?"* (Can this, somehow, be death?)

No decor; the scenery consists solely of pools of light whose varying color and intensity create an atmosphere that is both calm and mysterious.

Wir sind durch Not und Freude
Gegangen Hand in Hand,
Vom Wandern ruhn wir beide
Num überm stillen Land.

Through anguish and through pain
have we gone together, hand in hand,
and together will we rest from our wanderings
in the stilled landscape.

Can this be death?

The third woman

The second woman

Can this be death?

O weiter stiller Friede !
So tief im Abendrot
Wie sind wir wandermüde -
Ist das etwa der Tod ?

O vast, silent peace!
So bathed in sunset's glow,
We are weary of wandering,
Can this, somehow, be death?

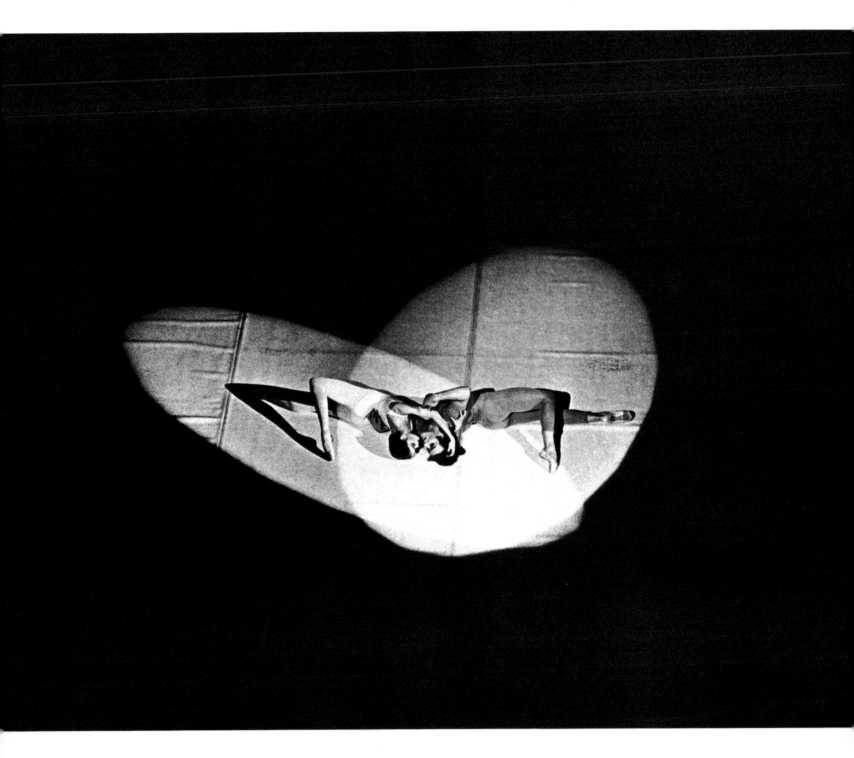

What Love Tells Me

Music by Gustav Mahler
Costumes by Judith Gombar

First performance,
December 24, 1974,
at the Opéra of Monte Carlo,
danced by:

Luciana Savignano	Angèle Albrecht
Jorge Donn	Dyane Gray-Cullert
Michel Gascard	Catherine Verneuil
	Patrice Touron
	Yvan Marko
	Andrzej Ziemski
	Bertrand Pie
	Jan Nuyts
	Gérard Wilk
	Niklas Ek
	Dwight Lomont-Hugues
	Iukihiko Sakai

Mahler's *Third Symphony* contains six movements, of which Béjart has used the last three. The ballet opens with "What the Night Tells Me," a contralto solo to a poem from Nietzsche's *Thus Spake Zarathustra,* a pure, calm, and solemn melody accompanied by a reduced orchestra.

The next movement, "What the Angels Tell Me," a setting of a poem from *Des Knaben Wunderhorn,* is a description of Heaven and Christ's pardon of Saint Peter. The contralto soloist is joined by a chorus of children's and women's voices.

The final movement, "What Love Tells Me," consists of an adagio in D major for full orchestra. In the initial theme, stated by the violins, Mahler expresses his basic inspiration: the music contains no conflict, even when earlier themes reappear, but breathes deeply and serenely, unhurried and almost religious in feeling—Mahler had at one point thought of giving this section the title "What God Tells Me"—and it soars to a striking and powerful climax.

The ballet begins with the man, naked and prostrate in the foreground; behind him, twelve enigmatic figures dressed in wide, heavy cloaks and wearing lofty coronets—twelve aspects of the night—who gradually withdraw to reveal the woman, dressed in white. Is she night itself, man's inspiration, or is she the harbinger of his future work? The man and the woman join in a pas de deux, after which she too withdraws.

Then the children—the angels?—appear and draw the man for a time into their joyous, carefree dance…in vain.

Alone once more at the front of the stage, the man sees the twelve figures from the ballet's opening reappear, one by one, now devoid of cloaks and coronets: they form a constellation around him, moving with increasing complexity as the music becomes more intense.

In the concluding section, the woman returns to join the man, finally offering to him—giving to him—as a complement to herself, one of the children—one of the angels—from the earlier section.

The twelve figures of the Night

Eins!
O Mensch! Gib acht!
Zwei!
Was spricht die tiefe Mitternacht?
Drei!
«Ich schlief, ich schlief-,
Vier!
«Aus tiefem Traum bin ich erwacht:
Fünf!
«Die Welt ist tief,
Sechs!
«Und tiefer als der Tag gedacht.
Sieben!
«Tief ist ihr Weh-,
Acht!
«Lust - tiefer noch als Herzeleid:
Neun!
«Weh spricht: Vergeh!
Zehn!
«Doch alle Lust will Ewigkeit!»
Elf!
«will tiefe, tiefe Ewigkeit!»
Zwölf!

One!
O Man, pay heed!
Two!
What does deep Midnight say?
Three!
"I wake, I wake…
Four!
…from a deep dream:
Five!
The world is deep∴
Six!
…and must be pondered more deeply than the day!
Seven!
Its grief is deep…
Eight!
…but joy is more profound than heartbreak."
Nine!
Sorrow says, "Pass by!"
Ten!
But Joy requires all of eternity…
Eleven!
…all of the vastness of eternity!
Twelve!

The Woman

*Musique des formes
qui épouse la musique des Sons.*

Music of shapes wed to the music of sound.

Partition pour l'œil ...
Le Temps devenu lisib[le]
recrée par l'intérieur.

A visual score... Time becomes writing,
space is recreated from within.

l'espace

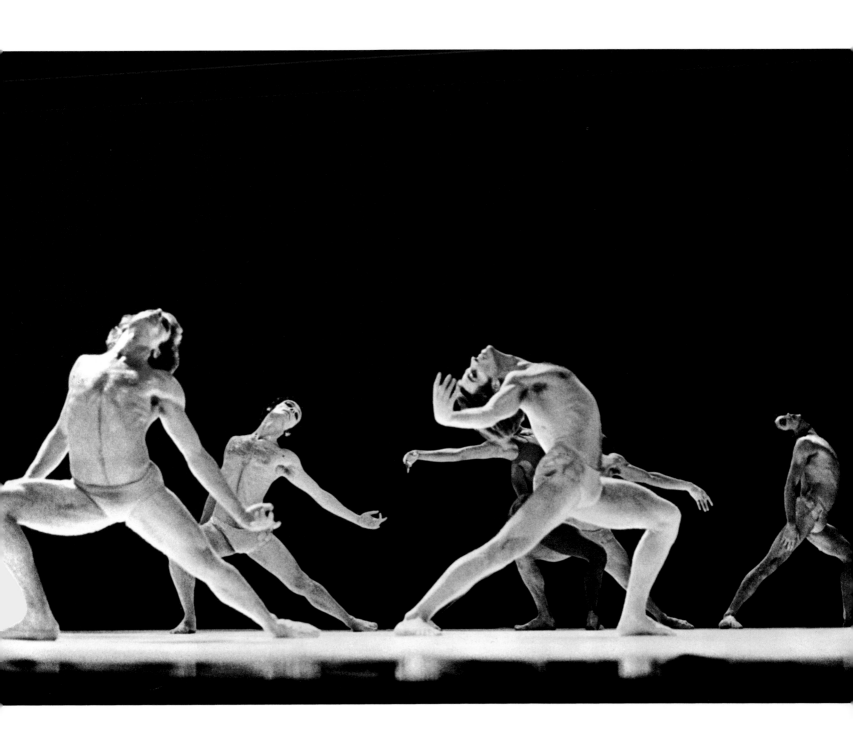

Golestan, or The Rose Garden

Based on a poem by Saâdi
Traditional Iranian music
Scenery and costumes by Joëlle Roustan
and Roger Bernard

First performance,
August 30, 1973,
at Persepolis,
with the following cast:

The Traveler   Alain Louafi
The Bearer of Light   Jorge Donn
The Mystic Rose   Suzanne Farrell

and the Ballet of the Twentieth Century

Although the Orient has been an uninterrupted source of inspiration for Béjart, the way in which he approaches it manifests the novelty of his attitude toward it.

He has never been tempted to indulge in the fairy-tale atmosphere of *Le Coq d'Or* and *Scheherazade;* the Japan of *Hi Kyo,* the India of *The Voyage* and *Bhakti,* the Persia of *Golestan* and *Farah,* are in no way picturesque. Instead, by employing age-old theatrical ritual, episodes in a spiritual journey, the trappings of ceremony and allegory, Béjart attempts to capture the very essence of a mode of thought, a poetry, a path of existence in the world.

The sensual and mystical side of Béjart is brought out by Saâdi. In this ballet, he enters into the Rose Garden in which the Persian poet glorifies God through the beauty of the visible world—above all through the faces and bodies of the young men and women he describes. From Saâdi's work, in which tales alternate with poems, moral fables with satire, Béjart has drawn material for a series of variations on the dual theme of dream and reality, the rose fragile and transient and the rose everlasting:

"A traveler lost in the desert suddenly sees a troop of men spring up around him.
Dream or reality?
They dance, and the traveler joins them in praising God through exalted and cosmic movement.
The wind rises
and each lies down upon the ground beneath his cloak in the darkness.
Suddenly, out of the storm, appears a wondrous Rose Garden
Reality or dream?
Attracted and fascinated, the men rise and enter the Garden smell the perfume of the flowers.
They are twelve.
Then the Bearer of Light appears and reveals to them the true rose, the mystic rose, SHE who will not fade.
The wind rises.
The vision of the Garden disappears.
The men dance in praise of God and go off into the desert.
The Traveler is left alone.
Dream or reality?"

In performances in Brussels and Paris, the stage was laid out in the form of a pointed arch, its apex toward the audience. A similar arch at the back of the stage served to frame the Iranian musicians.

The Traveler

A Sufi was rapt in deep meditation
on the Divine Presence; as he awakened
from his dream, his companions
asked him what miraculous gifts he had
brought back for them from the
garden of meditation to which he had
been transported. He replied:
"I had intended to fill my robe with roses
for you, but when I found myself
standing before the rose bush, the
odor of the flowers so intoxicated me
that I was unable to move."

Later, as we walked in the gardens,
he gathered flowers, and I said to him:
"Flowers do not last, and nothing
that does not last can merit devotion."
He asked: "What should I do, then?"
And I replied: "I shall make
for you a book, the Rose Garden,
and it will not perish."

The Bearer of Light

La Rose, qui est fleur, et
"
            Lumière su

me , et blessure mystique ...
Lumière ,,

The Rose, which is flower, flame,
and mystic wound…"Light upon Light"

LIGHT   En Anglais le même mot signifie Leger et Lumière

LIGHT   In English the same word means both "without weight" and "luminous"

Take a rose from the garden,
It will last but a few days,
Take a petal from my Rose Garden.
It will last throughout Eternity.

*"La pureté du vent
La clarté de la lune
Qui peut les peindre?.."*

anonyme Japonais.

"Who can depict the purity of the wind, the light of the moon?"

Anonymous Japanese writer

The Traveler

Per la Dolce Memoria di Quel Giorno

Inspired by *I Trionfi* by Francesco Petrarch
Music by Luciano Berio
Stage design and costumes by
Joëlle Roustan and Roger Bernard

First performance,
July 9, 1974,
in the Boboli Gardens in Florence,
with the following cast:

Laura	Suzanne Farrell
The Poet	Jorge Donn
The Poet's Friend	Daniel Lommel
The Woman	Angèle Albrecht
A Forest Spirit	Victor Ullate
Love	Bertrand Pie
The Unicorn	Rita Poelvoorde
Death	Patrice Touron
The Shadow	Dyane Gray-Cullert
The Two Faces of Time	Niklas Ek and Yvan Marko
The Phoenix	Jan Nuyts

The Ballet of the Twentieth Century
and the students of Mudra

Six episodes depict the poet's successive visions: Love, Chastity, Death, Fame, Time, Eternity. Chastity triumphs over Love, Death triumphs over Chastity, and so on.

The transitions from one episode to the next are made through five interludes led by a Forest Spirit and Nature Sprites, and these interludes also comment on each preceding episode.

The first four allegorical figures enter in chariots, as in traditional processions of the Middle Ages and the Renaissance: Love is naked, an antique God carrying a bow and arrow; Chastity, personified by Laura, appears with a Unicorn, the symbol of mischief and virgin purity; Death is disguised as a warrior and preceded by a forbidding shadow; Fame, heralded by the Phoenix, appears in the midst of trumpeters.

Time's entrance is quite different: it is represented by two figures, one of which appears mounted on stilts, wearing an immense cloak which hangs from its shoulders and covers the Hours. Each figure represents one aspect of Time: the cyclical aspect, suggesting the alternation of day and night, the eternal passage of the seasons; and the eschatological aspect, evoking the fate of man, his life as a succession of trials, stages in his journey toward a promised land.

Eternity, finally, is not represented by a single figure: all the dancers appear on stage without their costumes and gradually cease to move.

In Brussels and in Paris, the ballet was performed before a vast backdrop on which fragments of works by Botticelli were projected in rapid succession, with a whirlwind effect.

The Poet

Al tempo che rinnova i miei sospiri
per la dolce memoria di quel giorno
che fu principio a sì lunghi martiri,
　　già il Sole al Toro l'uno e l'altro corno
scaldava, e la fanciulla di Titone
correa gelata al suo usato soggiorno
　　Amor, gli sdegni e 'l pianto e la stagione
ricondotto m'aveano al chiuso loco
ov'ogni fascio il cor lasso ripone.

In the season that renews my longings
With the sweet memory of this day
That saw the beginning of my long martyrdom,
When the sun again warmed the two horns of
Taurus, and Titon's young bride
Returned trembling to her former home,
My tears, my sorrow, love, and the season
Brought me back to this enclosed space
Where my weary heart might find rest.

1. The Triumph of Love—*Trionfo d'Amore*

Ivi fra l'erbe, già del pianger fioco,
vinto dal sonno, vidi una gran luce
e dentro assai dolor con breve gioco
    Vidi un vittorioso e sommo duce
pur com'un di color che 'n Campidoglio
trionfal carro a gran gloria conduce.

Resting there upon the grass, weary with weeping
And overcome with sleep, I saw in the brilliant sunlight
That revealed so little joy and so much sorrow,
A victorious and magnificent hero,
Like those once drawn in a triumphal car
With glory to the Campidoglio.

Love

Love Conquered by Chastity

Costei non è chi tanto o quanto stringa,
così selvaggia e rebellante suole
da le 'nsegne d'Amor andar solinga :
    e veramente è fra le stelle un sole,
un singular suo proprio portamento,
suo riso, suoi disdegni e sue parole;
    le chiome accolte in oro o sparse al vento,
gli occhi ch'accesi d'un celeste lume
m'infiamman sì ch'i' son d'arder contento.

No person has power over her,
So rebellious is she to the yoke of Love,
Living unapproachable and ever cold.
She is like the sun among the stars
And her comportment is unlike all others:
Her smile, her disdain, her speech,
Her golden hair bound up or flying in the wind,
Her eyes that sparkle with celestial light—
All inflame me, and I am content to burn.

The pas de deux of Laura and the Poet

123

The Unicorn

The dance of Laura and the Unicorn

Interlude between the Triumph of Chastity and the Triumph of Death

3. The Triumph of Death—*Trionfo della Morte*

The Shadow of Death

Dance of Laura and Death

Lo spirto, per partir di quel bel seno
con tutte sue virtuti in sé romito,
fatto avea in quella parte il ciel sereno.
    Nessun degli avversari fu sì ardito
ch'apparisse già mai con vista oscura
fin che Morte il suo assalto ebbe fornito.

When it departed her glorious body
In which every virtue was mingled,
Her Soul made the sky more serene.
No thing that here below destroys beauty
Remained to tarnish her image or dim her radiance,
Until Death overcame her.

The Poet and the Shadow of Death

Interlude between the Triumph of Death and the Triumph of Fame

Nature Sprites

Pallida no ma più che neve bianca
che senza venti in un bel colle fiocchi,
parea posar come persona stanca :
*   quasi un dolce dormir ne' suo' belli occhi*
sendo lo spirto già da lei diviso,
era quel che morir chiaman gli sciocchi :
*   morte bella parea nel suo bel viso.*

No longer pale, but whiter still than snow
Lying upon a sheltered hillside,
She seemed to rest as though weary;
Asleep, as though sweet dreams had closed her eyes;
Lovely, as if her spirit had already departed.
And that is what we know as death—
Death too was lovely upon her face.

The Poet

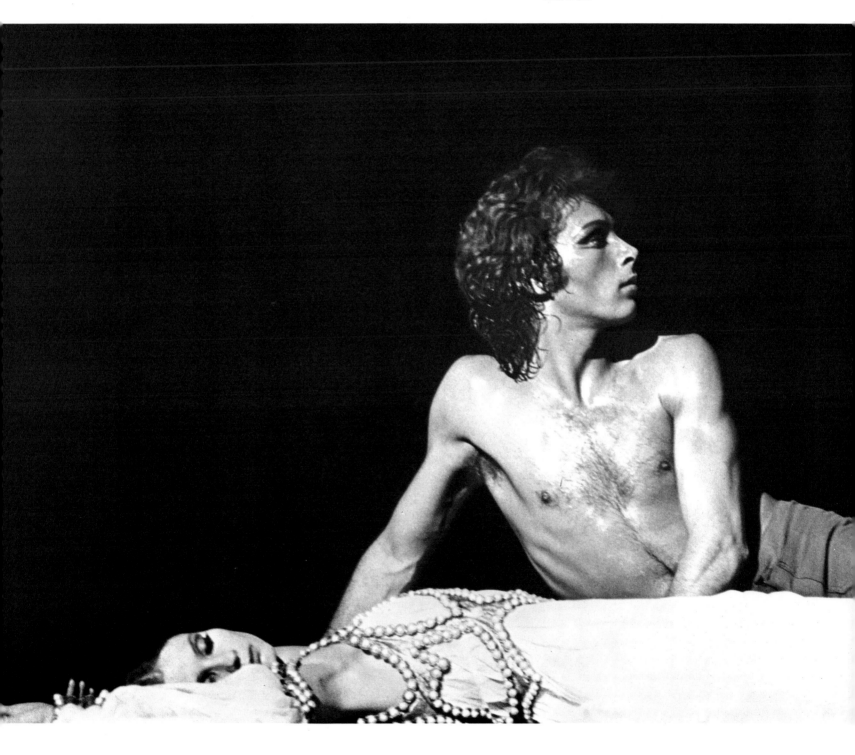

131

4. The triumph of Fame—*Trionfo della Fama*

Da poi che Morte trionfò nel volto
che di me stesso trionfar solea,
e fu del nostro mondo il suo sol tolto,
  partissi quella dispietata e rea,
pallida in vista, orribile e superba,
che 'l lume di beltate spento avea;
  quando, mirando intorno su per L'erba,
vidi da l'altra parte giugner quella
che trae l'uom del sepolcro e 'n vita il serba.

When Death triumphed over her who had triumphed over me,
When it had taken from our world her wondrous sun,
That cruel and pitiless creature departed,
Its visage pallid and awful, but with pride at
Having destroyed such luminous beauty.
Then, across the meadow, I saw appear that other one,
Who draws men from their tombs and returns them to life.

Fame, the Phoenix, Laura, and the Poet

The two incarnations of Time

The two incarnations of Time

Un dubbio inverno, instabile sereno,
è vostra fama, e poca nebbia il rompe,
e 'l gran tempo a' gran nomi è gran veneno.

    Passan vostre grandezze e vostre pompe,
passan le signorie, passano i regni :
ogni cosa mortal Tempo interrompe,
    e ritolta a' men buon, non dà a' piu degni;
e non pur quel di fuori il Tempo solve,
ma le vostre eloquenzie e' vostri ingegni.

Ah! your fame is like a fine but transient winter's day,
A mere cloud could destroy it, and vast time is
A great destroyer of great names.
Your glory and your pomp will pass,
Great lords will pass, reigns will fade away;
Time destroys all that is mortal,
It attacks the high and mighty as well as the lowly
            and unworthy,
Destroying not only your body, but your eloquence and genius.

"Le Temps est plus réel que li...
nous et lentement transforme
que l'espace n'est que le lien...

"Time is more real than space, because time is within us,
slowly altering and destroying our being, whereas space
is only the area within which phenomena occur." Gaston Berger

e , puisque le temps est en
t detruit notre être , alors
i se situent les phénomènes .,
mon père . Gaston Berger.

Fame conquered by Time

Qual meraviglia ebb'io quando ristare
vidi in un punto quel che mai non stette,
ma discorrendo suol tutto cangiare!

    E le tre parti sue vidi ristrette
ad una sola, e quella una esser ferma
sì che, come solea, più non s'affrette;

    e, quasi in terra d'erbe ignuda ed erma,
né « fia » né « fu » né « mai » né « innanzi » ó « 'ndietro »
ch'umana vita fanno varia e 'nferma!

    Passa il penser sì come sole in vetro,
anzi più assai, però che nulla il tene;
o qual grazia mi fia, se mai l'impretro,

    Ch'i' veggia ivi presente il sommo bene,
non alcun mal che solo il tempo mesce
e con lui si diparte e con lui vene!

How I marveled when I gazed on that which is ceaseless
And alters everything without motion.
I saw its three parts join into one unalterable entity,
And like a land emptied of creatures and growing things
Where no "now" or "then" or "ever" gives variation
Or solidity to human life.
And another thought came to me, more clearly
Than sunlight through crystal:
Oh, how happy would I be could I but contemplate
The Highest Good, free from all the sorrows Time creates,
Those sorrows it creates and that pass with it!

Nijinsky, Clown of God

Based on the *Journal* of Vaslav Nijinsky
Music by Pierre Henry
with extracts from Tchaikovsky's
Sixth Symphony (Pathétique)

Stage design and costumes by Joëlle Roustan
and Roger Bernard

First performance,
October 8, 1971,
in the Salle du Forest-National in Brussels,
with the following cast:

The Clown of God	Jorge Donn
The Rose	Paolo Bortoluzzi
The Golden Slave	Daniel Lommel
The Faun	Jörg Lanner
Petrouchka	Micha Van Hoecke
The Girl in Pink	Suzanne Farrell
The Nymph	Angèle Albrecht
The Society Woman	Jaleh Kerendi
The Ballerina	Catherine Verneuil
The Doll	Hitomi Asakawa
Auguste	Victor Ullate
The Pink Clown	Paul Mejia
The Golden Clown	Guy Brasseur
The Brown Clown	Franco Romano
The Blue Clown	Robert Denvers
Diaghilev	Pierre Dobriévich
Death	Dyane Gray-Cullert and Luc Bouy

Based on Nijinsky's *Journal,* the ballet consists of two sections: the Nijinsky of the Ballets Russes and the Nijinsky of God.

The first section forms a counterpoint to the story of Genesis: the Creation of the world and the Fall of Man.

Diaghilev, who is a giant marionette controlled by Monsieur Loyal, gives birth to the Clown of God. He teaches him to walk, leap, and dance. To keep him amused and under his control, Diaghilev creates the Earthly Paradise—the Ballets Russes—and provides him with four companions who are four reflections of himself.

But the Clown of God requires love: the ballerinas and the nymphs who populate Paradise fail to satisfy him, and so he turns to a poetic vision—the Girl in Pink.

This vision gradually takes form: girl becomes woman—his wife. Enraged, Diaghilev drives the pair from Paradise.

The second section of the ballet consists of a series of trials through which the Clown of God, alone, attempts to attain the true God, the God of love and forgiveness. Haunted at first by terrifying visions of Madness and Death, the Clown manages to drive them from his mind. He then rejoins his wife and her companions for one last time. They are unable to follow him further on his spiritual quest. Experiencing the sufferings of Christ, the youth crucifies himself and sees, while hanging upon the cross, apocalyptic visions: grotesque figures, disguised as a lawyer, a bishop, a general, a doctor, ballerinas wearing skull-like masks, nymphs transformed into prostitutes. Diaghilev, the giant marionette—his former god—then collapses, and the Clown of God nears the end of his journey. He is gradually absorbed into the inchoate and teeming masses of earthly creatures, while his double, the ever-present Auguste, places a single rose in his outstretched hand.

Monsieur Loyal,
The Clown of God,
Diaghilev

The Spectre of the Rose

The Golden Slave

Petrouchka

The Faun

The Vision of Love
or The Girl in Pink

The ever-present Auguste and the Clown of God

I am flesh and sensation,
without the intervention
of intelligence.

I am Nijinsky, who dies if he is not loved.

The Girl in Pink

Dans Nijinsky la Rose
rejoint la croix, le symbolisme
alchimique du Moyen-Age qui
à travers traditions chrétiennes
et Islamiques réunies ...

In Nijinsky, the Rose is
united with the cross, the
alchemistic medieval symbolism
that, in both the Christian
and the Islamic traditions...

I bought her roses,
and every day I would bring her
twenty of them.

nous offre un conte initiatique...

...represents for us an initiatory tale...

I am the sea-bird
and the bird that flies over the earth.

... où la folie n'est qu'une des

The Girl in Pink, the Clown of God, and his four reflections, Air, Fire, Earth, and Water

Divine Love

mes de la connaissance véritable...

...in which madness is merely one of the modes of true knowledge...

The Clown of God and the four Clowns: the Pink, the Gold, the Brown, and the Blue

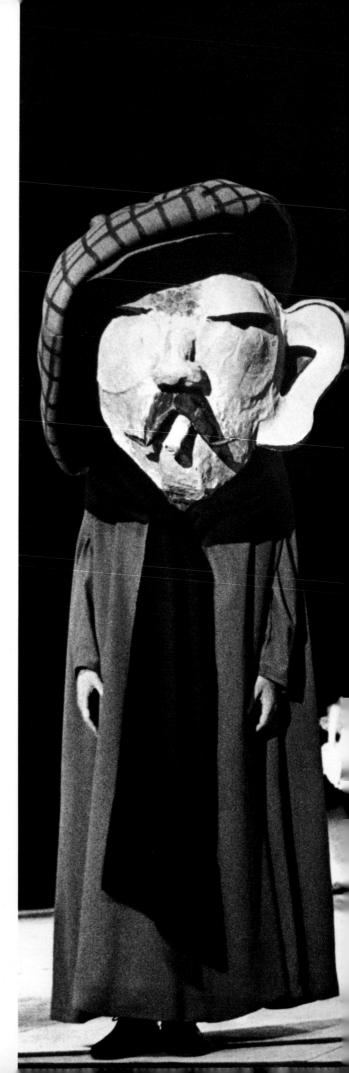

I am God made man,
    and I experience what Christ suffered.

... Les Fous de Dieu qui partaien

...the Holy Madmen who set out barefoot on the
Crusades join with the desert hermits and the sufis...!
As did Nijinsky, El Hallaj, the great saint of Islam,
said: "I am God" (he was crucified)!

Agony

mes pieds
aux croisades,
rejoignent

ermites du désert

et Soufis ...! — Comme Nijinsky
le grand saint de l'Islam

l HALLAJ

disant :

My little girl began to sing:
She sings, "Ah, ah, ah, ah."
What can she be trying to say?
I sense that for her the sounds mean:
"Ah, ah, there is no horror—Everything is Joy!"

" Je suis Dieu ..
(il fut crucifié) !

Le Molière Imaginaire*

Music by Nino Rota
Scenery and costumes by Joëlle Roustan
and Roger Bernard

Ballet-play first performed
December 3, 1976,
at the Comédie-Francaise, Paris

The photographs, taken at the
first performance and during the revival
in 1977, show the following cast:

Death	Elizabeth Cooper
The Actor	Maurice Béjart or Robert Hirsch
Scaramouche	Jean-Michel Bouvron
Armande	Shonah Mirk
Mademoiselle Menou	Virginie Lommel
Harlequin, the Marquis	Patrice Touron
The Young Molière	Bertrand Pie
Agnès	Rita Poelvoorde
Les Précieuses Ridicules	Maguy Marin and José Parès
Apollo, The King	Jorge Donn
Tartuffe	Yann Le Gac

The bare stage of a theater. At center stage, an armchair, the same as in *Le Malade Imaginaire*. At the front of the stage, on the left, a piano. Dim lighting. At the back of the stage, Death appears—could she be Madame de Maintenon? She crosses the stage and sits down at the piano. A contemporary actor enters. Gradually, led by Scaramouche, he begins to turn into Molière.

Thus begins a play based on Molière's life and work; the osmosis between one and the other is such that each character is doubled: Armande-Mademoiselle Molière is Célimène; Catherine-Mademoiselle de Brie is Agnès; La Grange is Apollo—that is, the King. The actors of Molière's life perform scenes taken from his plays: the dialogue between Cléonte and Covielle in *Le Bourgeois Gentilhomme* becomes a portrait of Armande.

So, too, his life recalls his work: Armande re-creates Agnès. However, Agnès appears disguised as a bear in pursuit of Moron, the coward in *La Princesse d'Elide*—and Moron in turn becomes Arnolphe, with the help of Agnès. As counterpoint, we have the famous scene from *L'Ecole des Femmes,* which begins: "What a lovely walk." "Very lovely."

The adult Molière performs with Mademoiselle Menou, who becomes Armande as a child. The author naturally recites Arnolphe's speech to the child: "She would reply: 'a custard pie.' " Whereupon Mascarille, out of *La Critique de l'Ecole des Femmes,* enters with his line: "Custard pie—egad!"

And so on.

The action becomes increasingly outrageous: the Précieuses Ridicules sing a Rossini aria; the King descends, like Apollo, in a stage machine and dances naked; Tartuffe attempts to lead Molière in a *valse noble et sentimentale;* doctors escaped from a Toulouse-Lautrec drawing dance a cancan like La Goulue—while Death, playing the piano or emerging from a coffin-shaped sedan chair, bides her time, crafty, watchful, and patient.

But the performance ends on a light note: Molière is alive. He has been saved from the pedants and is caught up in the whirlpool of a comedy-ballet—or ballet-comedy—for here, as throughout, dance predominates.

*Literally, "The Imaginary Molière"; a play on Molière's *Le Malade Imaginaire (The Imaginary Invalid;* i.e., hypochondriac).

Death

Molière, c'est la véritable aventure théâtrale, la Troupe, l'équipe, la famille artisanale, le Génie qui crée pour les autres, avec les autres —

Molière is true theatrical adventure, the Troupe, the tea...
the family of co-workers, the genius who creates for others, with othe...

Scaramouche   The Actor

Armande

In the end, however,

she is just as capricious

as everyone else.

Sganarelle

The Nurse

What a lovely walk.

Very lovely.

What a fine day!

Very fine.

Any news?

The kitten has died.

Agnès   Arnolphe

I would wish she were so naive
that if one chanced to play a
rhyming game with her,
and asked, "What's in my basket?"
she would reply: "A custard pie."

Mademoiselle Menou

Les Précieuses
Ridicules

Custard pie
egad!

The
Marquis

Apollo

I imagined a play about a poet,
whom I would have played myself, who would come to submit
a play to a troupe of actors...

Molière and his troupe

And which of you plays
the King's parts?

I'm an actor
who takes them
on sometimes.

Who? A well set-up
young man like yourself?
Are you joking?

Tartuffe

Marquises, snobs, cuckolds, doctors,
all have suffered their portrayals with good grace
and have even seemed amused, along with everyone else,
at the portraits drawn of themselves... but hypocrites have missed the joke...

Make an effort to seem faithful,
And I will make an effort to believe you are.

Armande—Célimène

Egad, must I love you!

Savantissimi doctores
Medicinae professores

The Doctors

Clysterium donare

Posta seignare

Ensuitta purgare

Isn't there

some risk

in feigning death?

Louis XIV—Molière

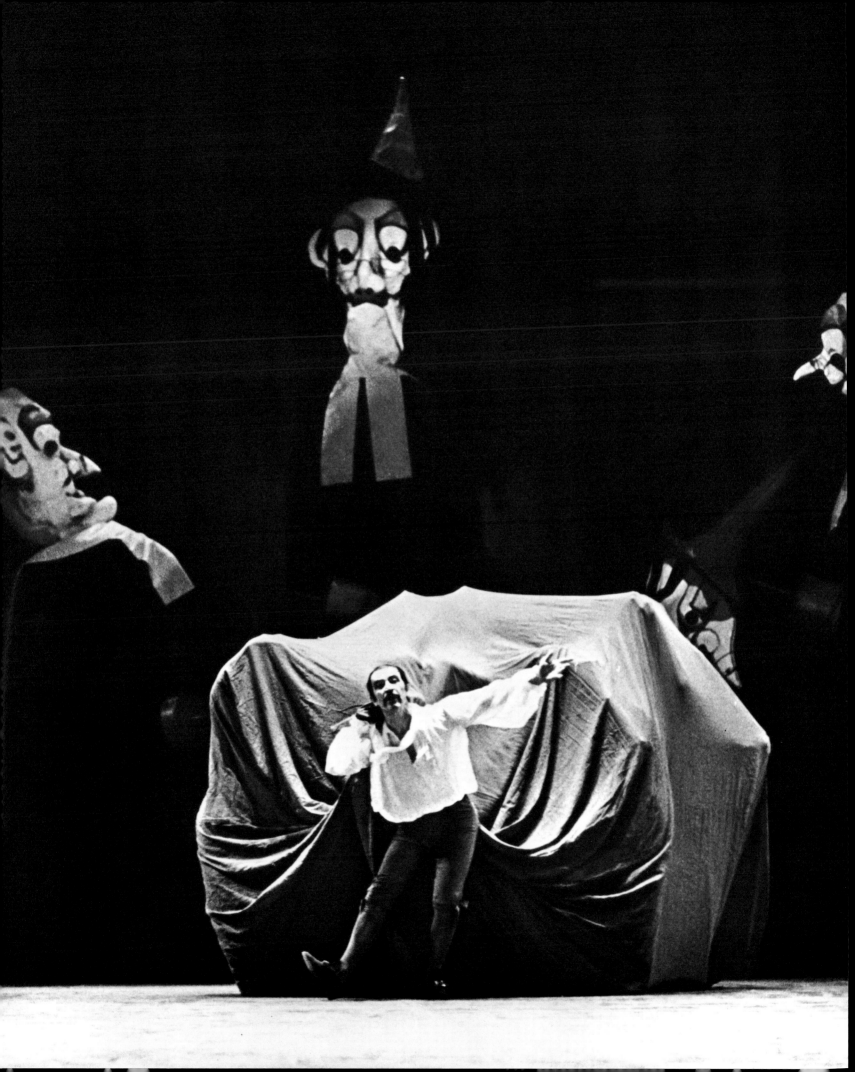

Our Faust

Variations on a theme by Johann Wolfgang Goethe
Music by Johann Sebastian Bach, with Argentine tangos

Scenery and costumes by Thierry Bosquet

First performance,
December 12, 1975,
At the Théâtre Royal de la Monnaie of Brussels,
with the following cast:

The Archangel Lucifer	Jorge Donn
The Archangel Satan	Bertrand Pie
The Archangel Beelzebub	Patrice Touron
The Aged Faust	Maurice Béjart
(who becomes Mephistopheles)	
Marguerite	Monet Robier
The Mother	Catherine Verneuil
Mephistopheles	Yann Le Gac
(who becomes the Young Faust)	
Helen of Troy	Shonach Mirk
The Child Faust	Maguy Marin

and the Ballet of the Twentieth Century

Goethe himself despised exegetes. "They ask me what idea I intended to personify in my Faust. As if I knew! Heaven and Hell, and all the world between! There, if you must, is a definition, but it is not an idea, it is the course the action takes."

The course the action takes: Béjart has used this as a point of departure for a series of "variations." The spectacle he creates is not a ballet but an immense black mass, in which the trappings and rites of Catholic liturgy are employed to accentuate the infernal subversion motivating the action. The work unfolds within a confined space, both cathedral and palace, inhabited by a vast, diffuse, and often overwhelming divine presence embodied in the Bach B minor Mass, brutally interrupted from time to time by Argentine tangos, trashy, violent music that enhances Mephistopheles' sarcasm and defiance—the spirit of eternal denial.

Béjart's "variations" deal with the unfolding of events in the play, the nature and role of its characters, and the ultimate meaning of the tragedy. A first variation concerns Mephistopheles himself, who appears as a "poor devil" controlled by three superiors who are none other than the three archangels Lucifer, Satan, and Beelzebub. They first appear disguised as bishops, the better to emerge later in all their nakedness—and beauty. One after the other, they offer Faust intoxication, wealth, and love, before conducting him to the Sabbath. A second variation concerns Marguerite and Helen of Troy. They appear to Faust as distant and unattainable creatures, for Mephistopheles assumes their features, their voices, and Faust is able to embrace no more than a magical simulacrum.

A third variation concerns the episode of the "Mothers"—the enigmatic passage in Part Two of the Goethe drama, in which Mephistopheles himself trembles at the mere mention of their name. The Aged Faust sees himself as a child with "his" mother. From this scene on, the spectacle acquires a tone so personal that Béjart appears to be confiding in his audience under the thin guise of fiction. Faust dies, Faust is reborn as on the first day, and the Archangel Lucifer again appears to him and raises him to the heights to the music of the Agnus Dei.

In the beginning was the Act

The Aged Faust

Habe nun, ach! Philosophie, Juristerei und Medizin,
Und leider auch Theologie
Durchaus studiert, mit heissem Bemühn.
Da steh' ich nun, ich armer Tor!
Und bin so klug als wie zuvor.

Beware! Philosophy, law, medicine,
and theology as well—unfortunately—
all of these I studied carefully,
and now you see me, a poor old fool,
knowing no more than I did when I began.

Six Adolescent Fausts (the pupils)

For years I have been leading my pupils
around by the nose.
    They call me "Master."
        What a joke!

The Aged Faust and the Twelve Adolescent Fausts

The Aged Faust and Mephistopheles

If I can say to the fleeting moment:
    Stay! you are so lovely—
then you may have me in your toils.

The Archangel Lucifer

197

Satan   Lucifer   Beelzebub

The Young Faust and Mephisto
wearing the mask of Marguerite

In the beginning was Love

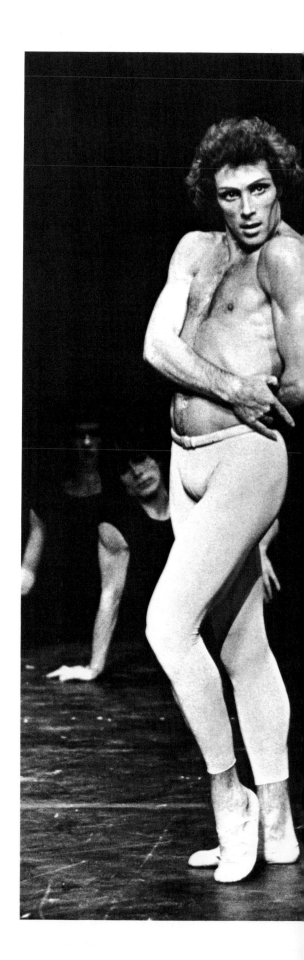

Mephisto

She is condemned!

She is saved!

Lucifer

In the beginning was Beauty

Euphorion, the new Icarus

Helen of Troy

The Mother

The Child Faust

Loves of a Poet

Music by Robert Schumann and Nino Rota
Poems by Heinrich Heine
Text by Charles Baudelaire
Costumes by Thierry Bosquet
Scenery and lighting by Alan Burrett

First performance,
December 4, 1978,
at the Palais des Beaux-Arts of Brussels,
with the following cast:

The Poet	Jorge Donn
The Woman in White	Andrzej Ziemski
The Man in Black	Jan Nuyts
Pegasus	Christian Dedeene
Angel	Yann Le Gac
The Girl	Rita Poelvoorde
The Cat	Bertrand Pie
George Sand	Catherine Verneuil
Dionysus	Jean-Marie Limon
Zarathustra	Patrice Touron

The ballet draws its inspiration from two sources: the *Dichterliebe* (Loves of a Poet), Schumann's song cycle to poems by Heine, and various musical scores composed for Fellini films by Nino Rota.

Passing through solitude, love, and sorrow while obeying the call of his dreams, fantasies, and desires, the Poet transforms his obsessions into a series of visible metaphors that can be grouped into four categories. First, his Friends: three Muses of tradition, who appear as Balanchine-inspired dancers, a furtive and playful Cat, and the image of his Beloved, a distant and unattainable Girl. Next come the Forces of Death: the Man in Black, a funereal Monsieur Loyal representing Anxiety; the Woman in White, enigmatic, changeable, danced by a man; Angel, the motorcyclist. Joining them are the mythological characters: Pegasus, Dionysus, Zarathustra—poetry, intoxication, and the dance. Lastly, ridiculous figures make their appearance: clowns, punchinellos, and George Sand as an old-time cabaret star. The poet—that is, the dancer—a classical dancer under the influence of Heine and Schumann—becomes a pierrot, a music-hall performer, a tramp, a clown, as the Forces of Death work upon him, inspire him, stimulate him, and soothe him: the Man in Black unleashes fantasy, the Woman in White suggests compassion, Angel dons the wings of Pegasus.

In the circus, at the height of the revels, these metamorphoses end when a little boy hands the clown a fateful pistol; surprised, resigned, the clown puts the pistol to his head and pulls the trigger, but the silent shot wipes out all save himself. The poet emerges from the clown disguise and finds himself faced once again with solitude—and eternity.

La mort ... dans ce ballet
où elle a 3 visages (Ballerine étrange,
Mr Loyal maléfique et l'ange -
Motard) n'est pas forcément ...

Death... in this ballet, in which it has three face
(a strange ballerina, the malevolent Monsieur Loya
and the angel-motorcyclist) is not necessaril

The Woman in White   The Man in Black

Pegasus

...l'ennemie du
La Mort est l[e]
grande sourc[e]
d'inspira[tion]

...the poet's enemy. Death is the greatest source of inspiration.

Angel

The Motorcyclists

La Mort
aussi
est
AMOUR ...

Death is also LOVE…

The Woman in White

The Girl

"Dans ma cervelle se promène, ainsi qu'en son appartement UN CHAT ...."

"In my brain there stalks, as in its home, A CAT..."

George Sand

The Punchinellos

The Woman in White 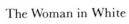 The Poet

The Poet's Coffin

Dionysus

Angel and
the wings
of Pegas

The Woman
in White

KALi en Inde est a Mort... mais aussi: LA MÈRE! La mort est Amour -

...dia, KALI is death... but also the MOTHER! Death is love.

The Poet as Clown

The Poet's Eternity

Silence

Documents

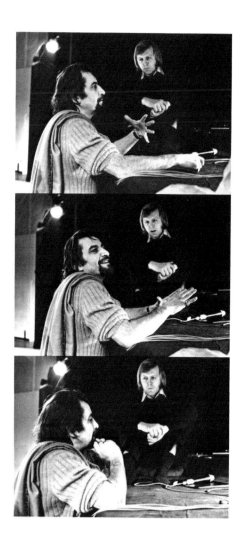

Rehearsal
Make-up
Performing Space
Lighting

During a rehearsal of *Stimmung,*
Maurice Béjart and Wolfgang Fromme, conductor of
the Collegium Vocale of Cologne

La Chorégraphie se fait
à deux, comme l'Amour.

It takes two to create
choreography, like making love.
Through the labyrinth of
another's body, I find the path
of my own thought, which
is nothing but forms and rhythms
and feelings and emotions.

Catherine Verneuil

A Travers le labyrinthe du
corps de l'autre, je trouve
le cheminement de ma
propre pensée qui n'est que
formes et rythmes et senti-
ments et émotions.

Rehearsal at Mudra (Brussels)
of *What Love Tells Me*
prior to the ballet's first performance
at the Opera of Monte Carlo

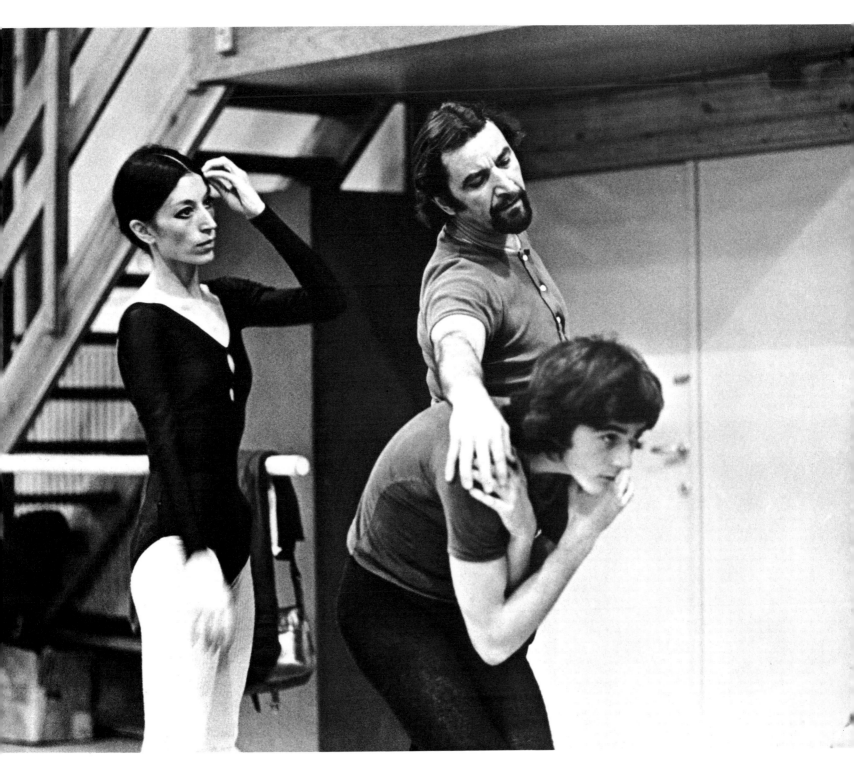

Luciana Savignano   Michel Gascard

Luciana Savignano

Jorge Donn

Andrzej Ziemski

Ivan Marko

Avoir des courbatures, endurer, transpirer, détruire et reconstruire le corps ... continuer ...

SANS CESSE

ne must suffer aches and pains, endure, sweat, destroy and rebuild the body... go on... UNCEASINGLY

Le mot sanscrit " MUDRA "
signifie "gestes" ; la pensée
faite chair, l'expression
abstraite de l'âme qui

During the presentation of *Golestan* in Paris

live le petit doigt et revèle
le pouvoir des signes, le
tangible qui est temoin
vivant de l'inexprimable

The Sanskrit word MUDRA means "gestures"; thought made flesh, the abstract expression of the soul that moves
the little finger and reveals the power of signs, the tangible that becomes the living witness of the inexpressible.

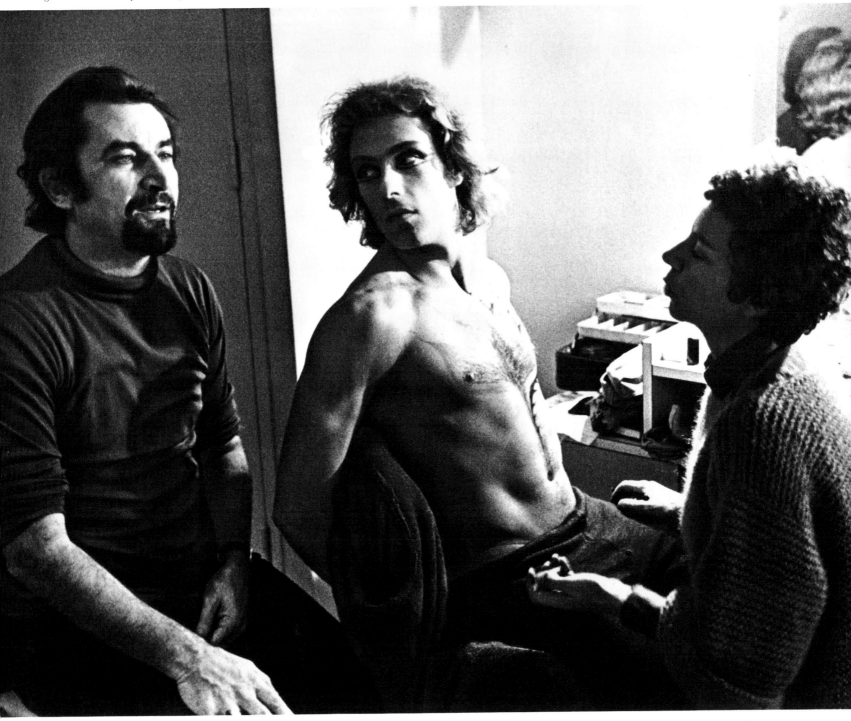

Maurice Béjart   Jorge Donn   Joëlle Roustan

La pensée souvent nous
égare   Dans le miroir
qui est devant moi, recherche
de l'autre moi-même.

Mon corps.

Je Danse donc je suis.

Joëlle Roustan outlines the scarlet flower of the Bearer of Light on Jorge Donn's chest.

Thought often leads us astray. To seek in the mirror
before me the other I.
   My body.
I dance, therefore I am.

Scenic space in the Boboli Gardens
I Trionfi in Florence

Scenic design by Joëlle Roustan and Roger Bernard

Conceived for an open space—the Boboli Gardens—the ballet was later produced indoors in the Palais des Congrès in Paris. In Florence, the trees, shrubbery, and statues formed an integral part of the decor. In Paris, the designer created a vast cyclorama in front of which the performance took place. Compare the photograph on the facing page with the photograph on pages 142–143.

La nature.
Le naturel.
Surnaturel.
Sur la nature, Je
Danse.

Attention le plein air est impitoyable et l'arbre voit bien ridiculisa tout geste qui ne fait pas du véritable centre de l'être.

Nature
The natural
Supernatural
Super-nature, upon nature, I
Dance
Beware, the open air is pitiless and a tree may well make ridiculous any gesture that is not founded in the true center of the human being.

*Formes, lignes, et souffle
et lumières.*

Forms, lines, and breathings and lights.

Golestan

The Mystic
Rose

The Bearer
of Light

The Vision
of the Garden

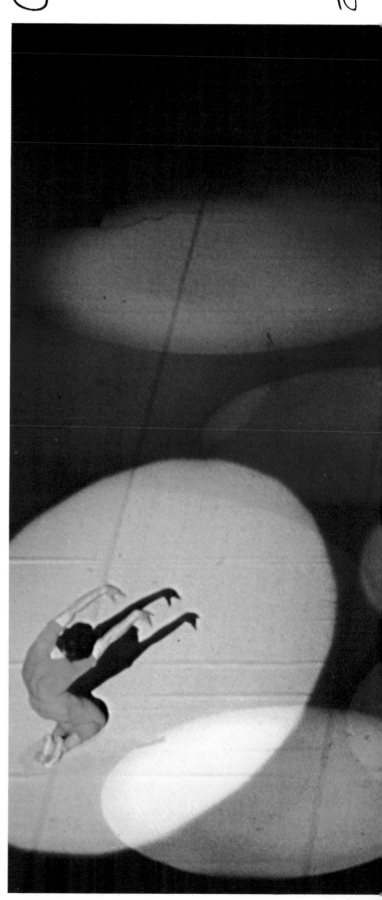

Can This Be Death? at the Palais des Congrès in Paris

Venise et la Danse ont
des points communs, et ce
rêve de pierre posé sur
l'eau rythme du temps
et de l'espace, sans pesanteur,
me fait sentir les limites
et les pouvoirs illimités
de ce corps qui se déploient
dans l'espace géométrique.

Venice and the Dance exist on a common ground, and this
dream in stone, set upon the water, rhythmic in time and
space, without weight, enables me to grasp the limits
and the limitless powers of this body that deploys
itself within geometric space.

First performed at the Cirque Royale in Brussels,
the ballet was danced ten years later, outdoors,
in Venice. The circular ground design used at
the Cirque Royale was changed to a design using
hexagons in order to complement the orthogonal
architecture of the Piazza San Marco.
Compare the photograph on the facing page with
the photographs on pages 42 and 43.

Scenic design by Joëlle Roustan and Roger Bernard

Contents

This book, part of the *Musiques et Musiciens* collection
directed by Odile Cail, was completed during the month of
September 1979.
Phototypesetting: Bussières Arts Graphiques
Reproduction: Roto-Sadag, Geneva for black/white artwork
using the helio-offset process
Grapholec, Paris for the colour artwork
Paper: Rochat, Geneva
Printing: Roto-Sadag, Geneva
Binding: Brun, Malesherbes
Technical Management: Jean-Pierre Courtin

Editor No. 79087
Legal deposit fourth quarter nineteen hundred and seventy-nine

Printed in Switzerland